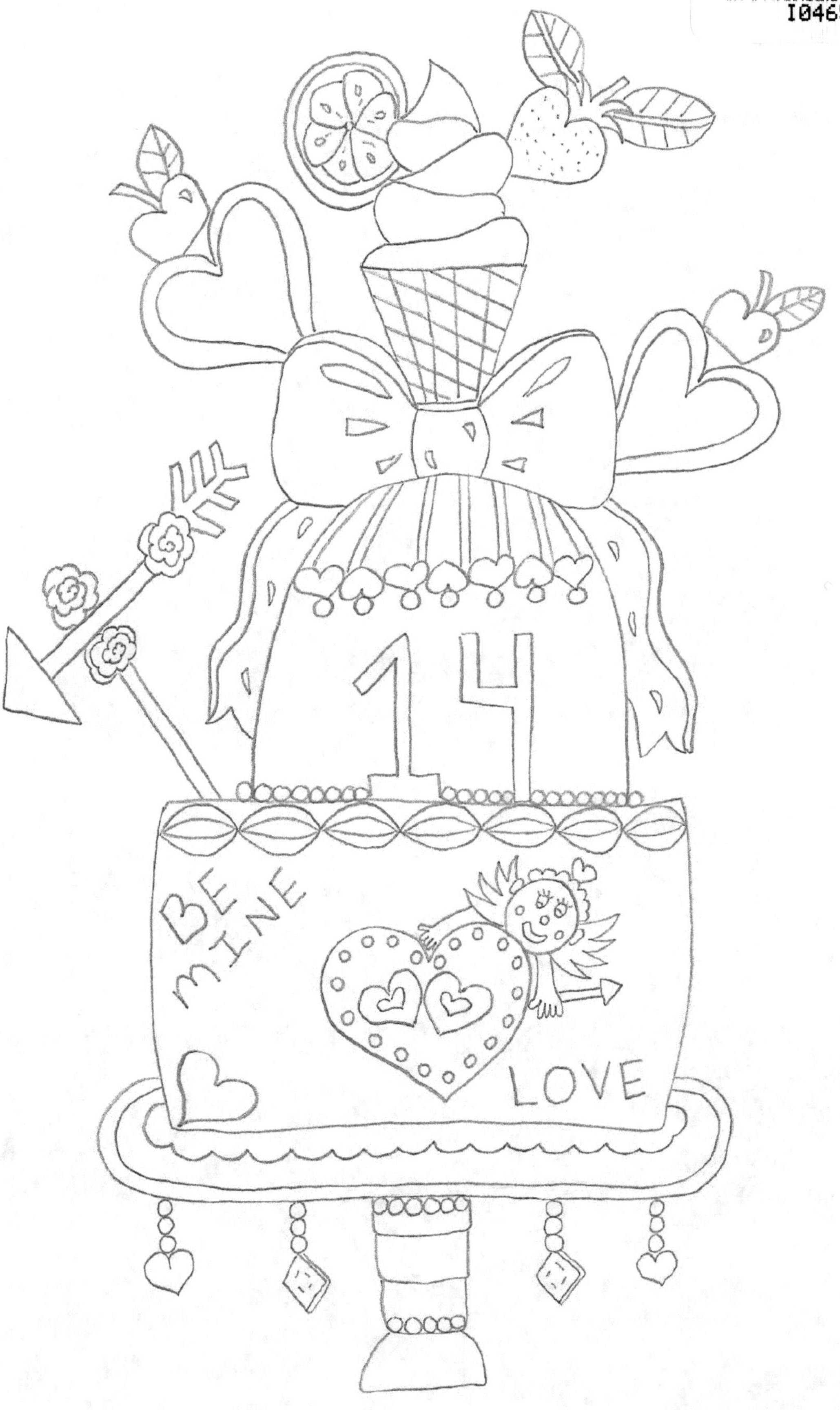

I0465971

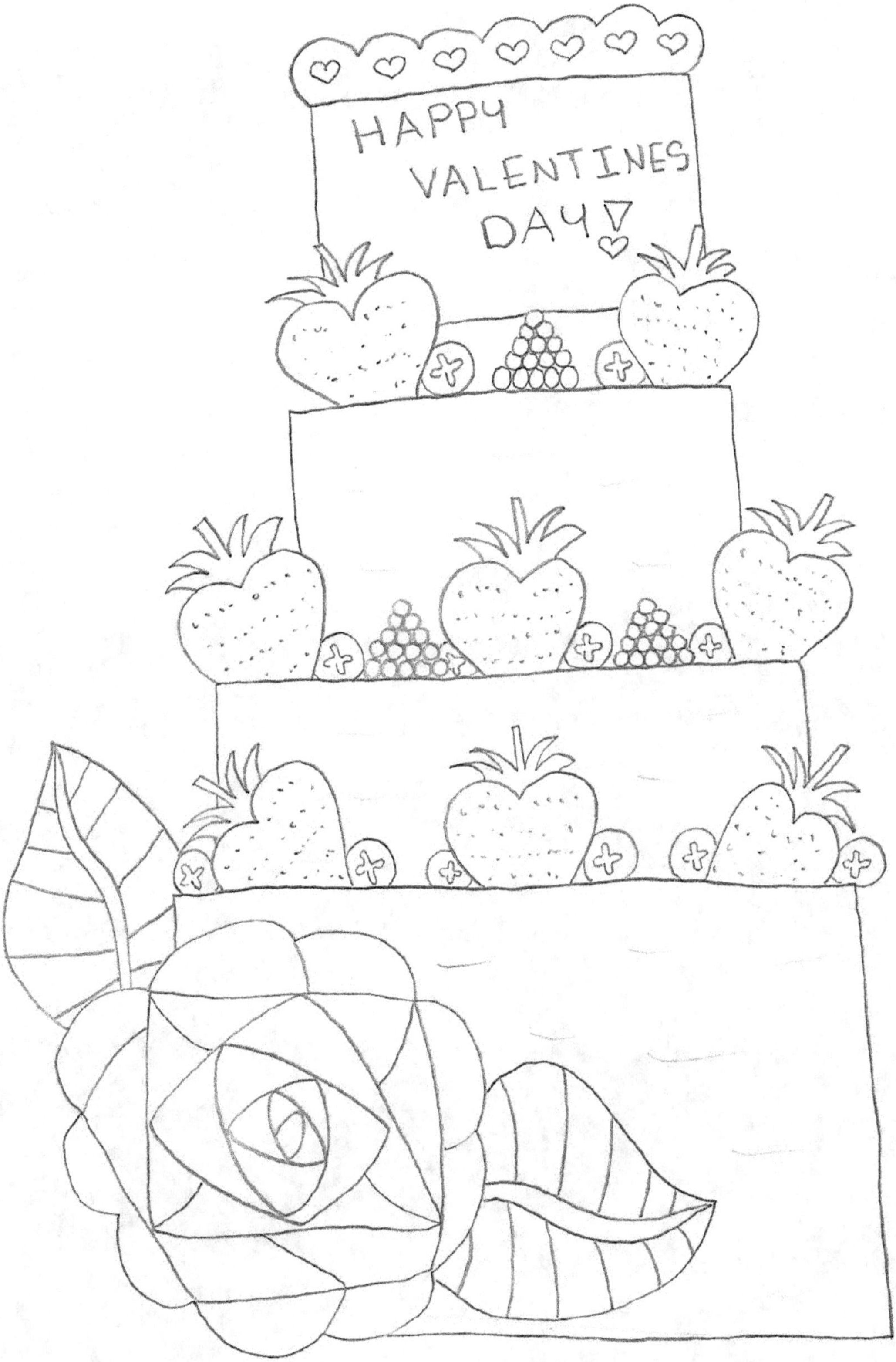
HAPPY
VALENTINES
DAY

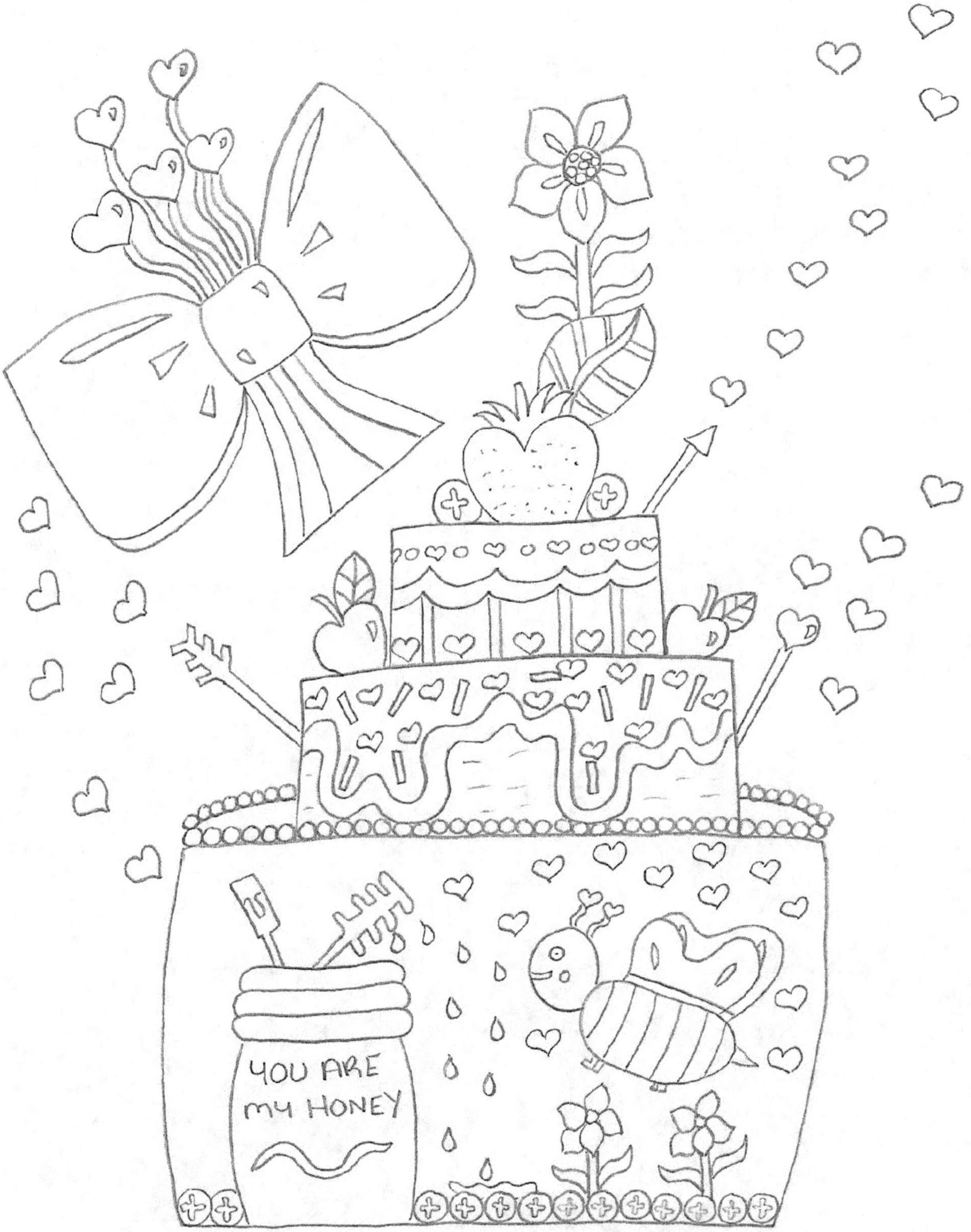
YOU ARE
my HONEY

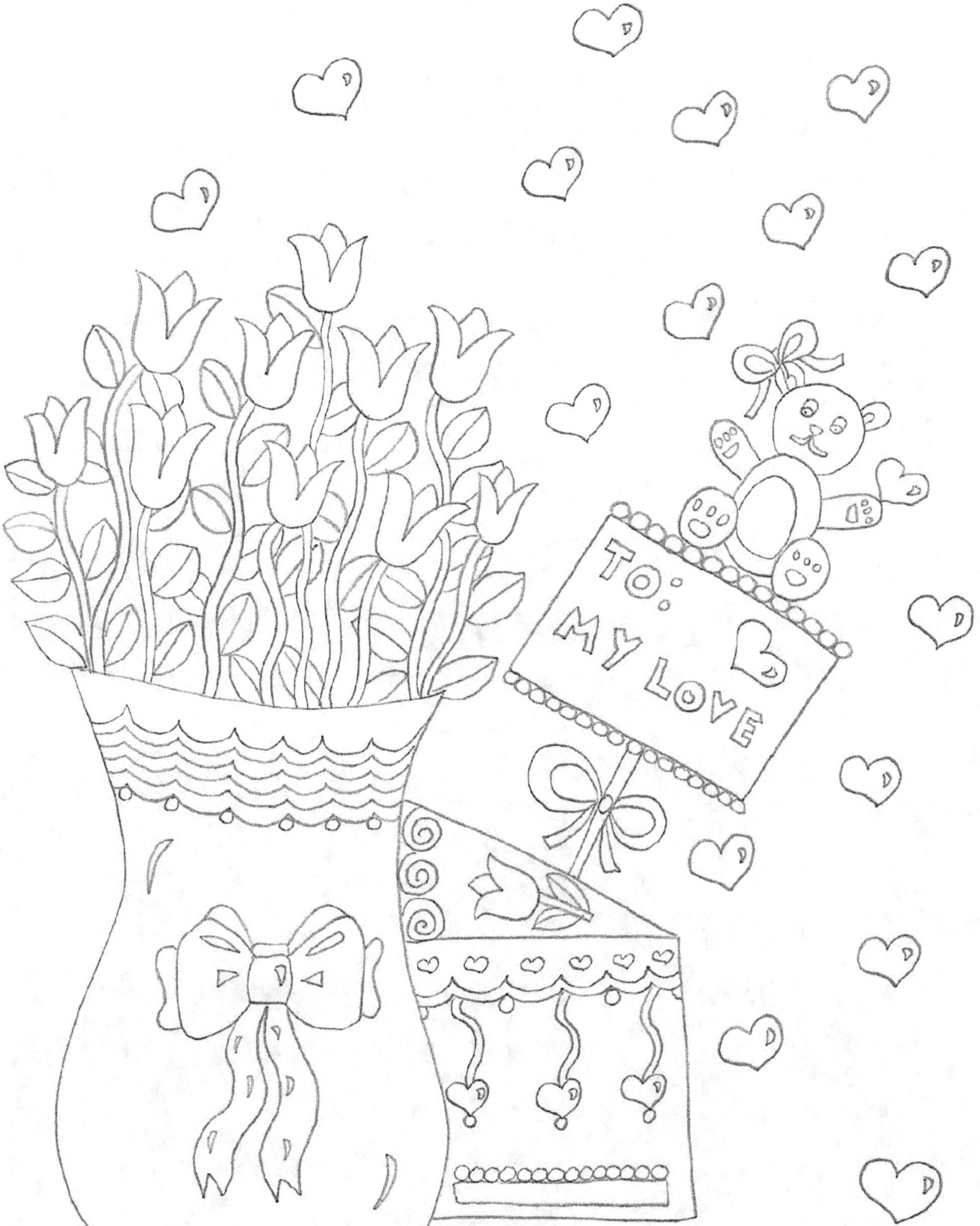
TO:
MY LOVE

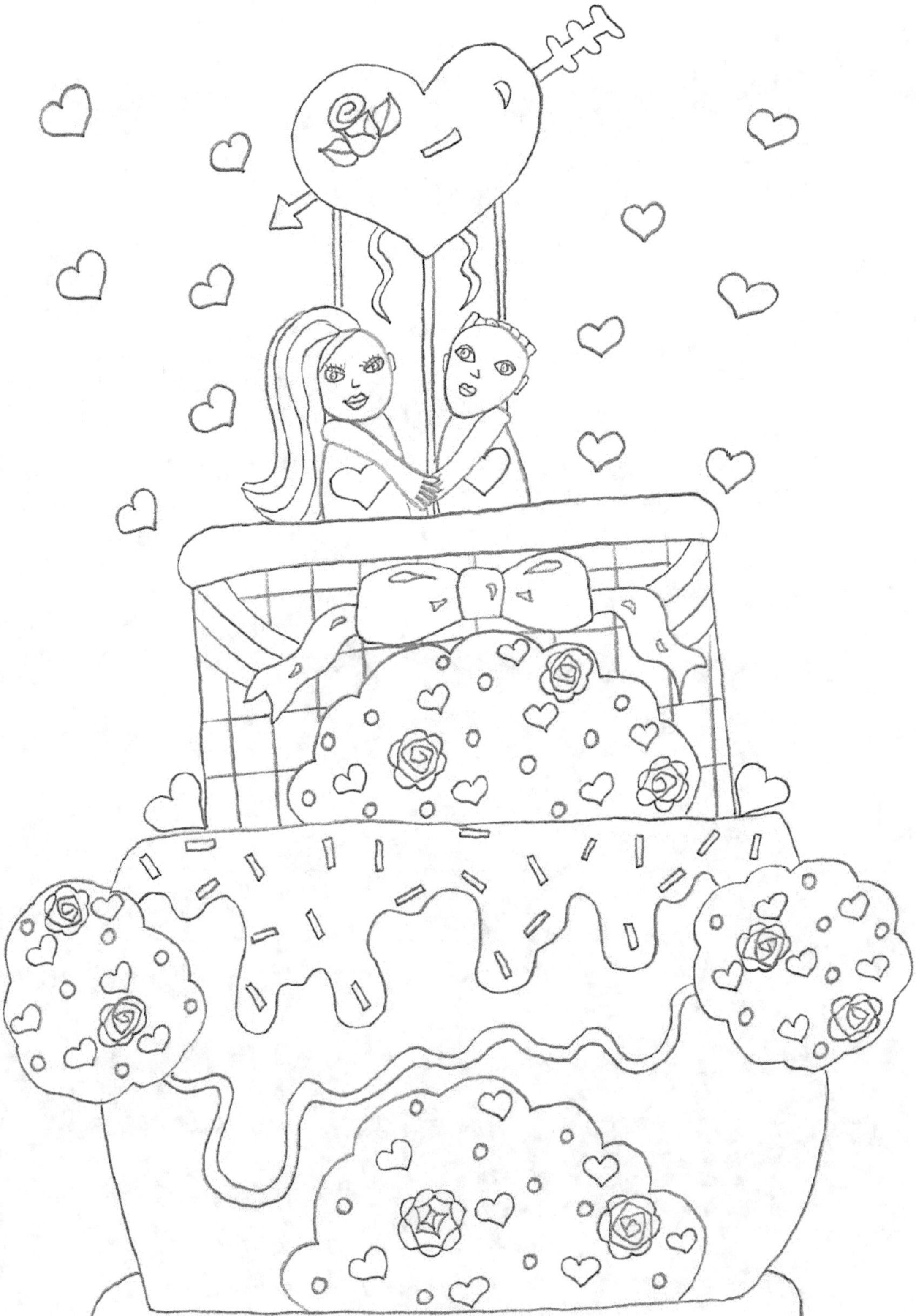

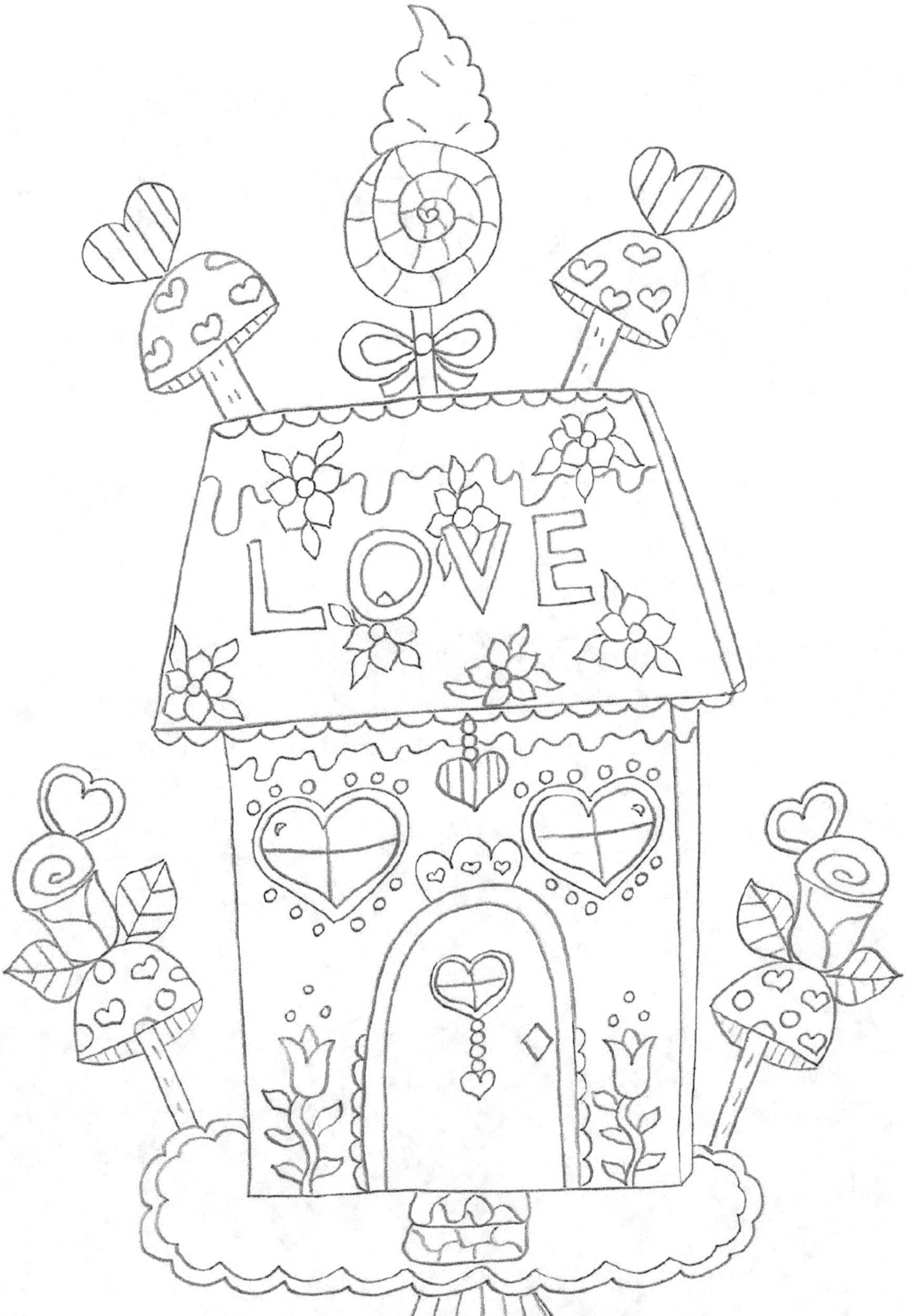
LOVE

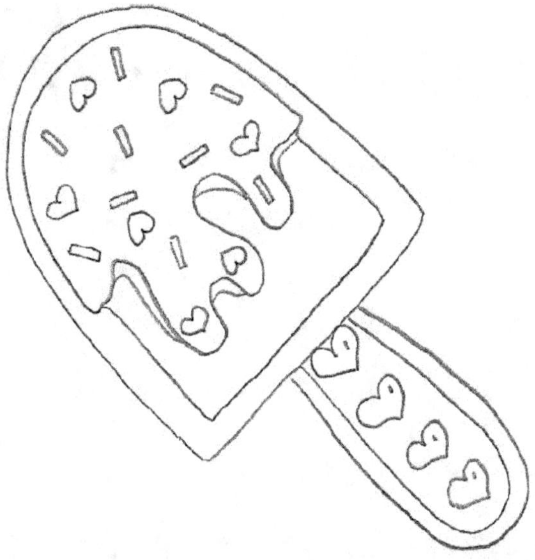

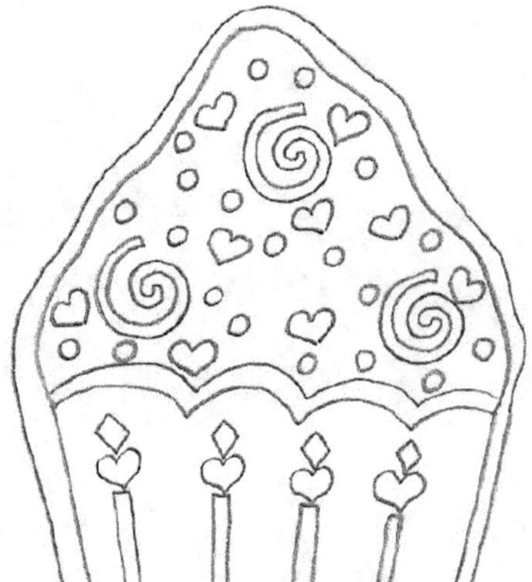

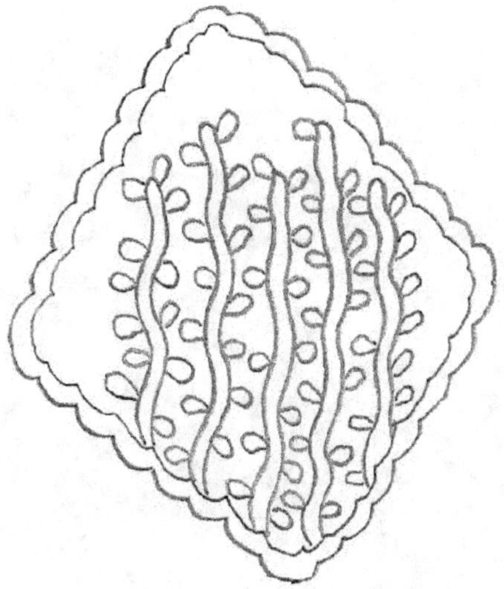

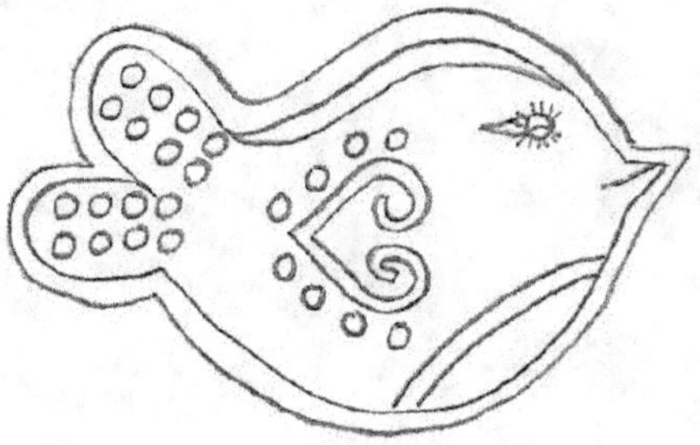

CUPID

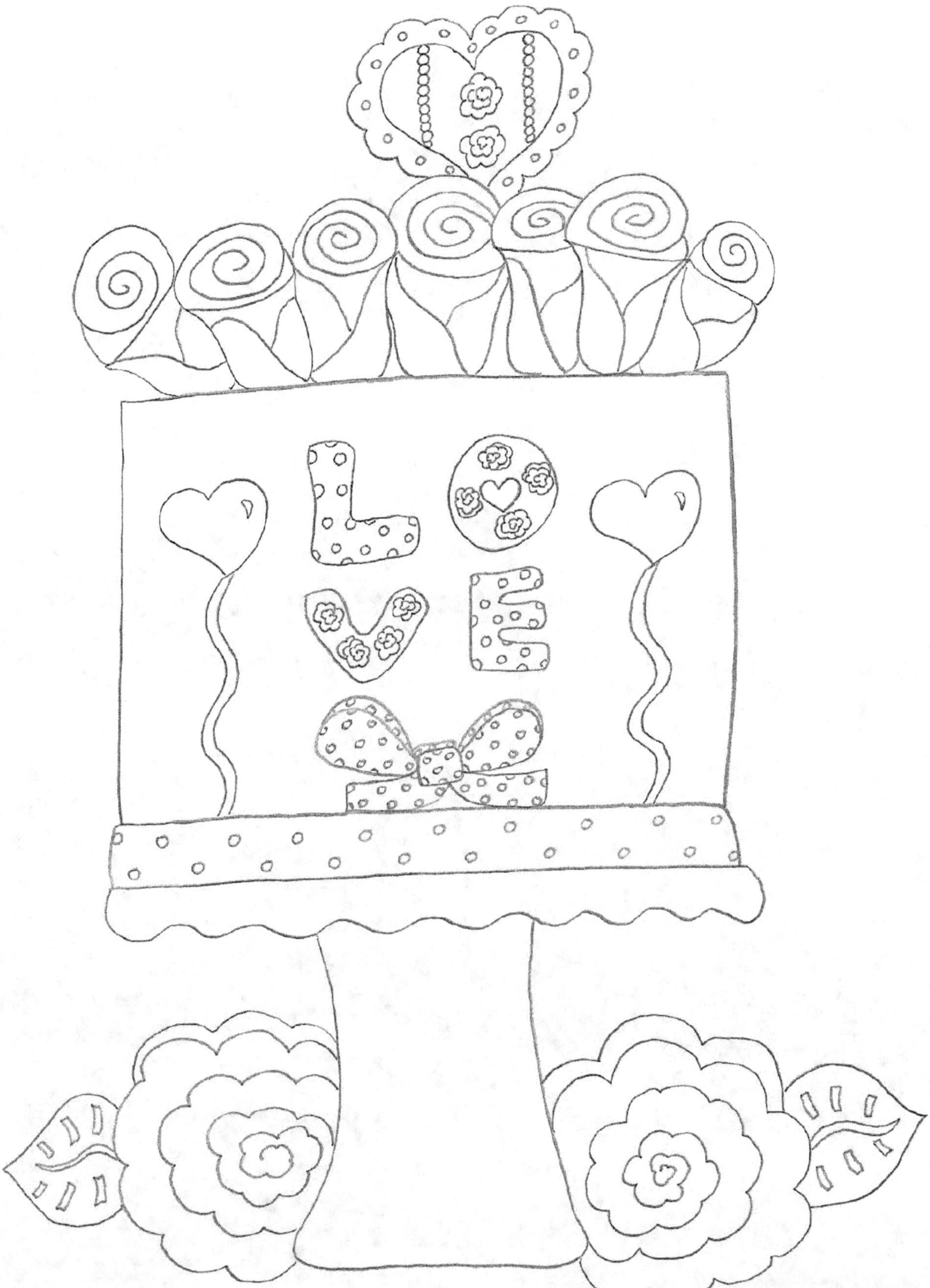
LOVE

COOKIES
HAPPY VALENTINES DAY
LOVE

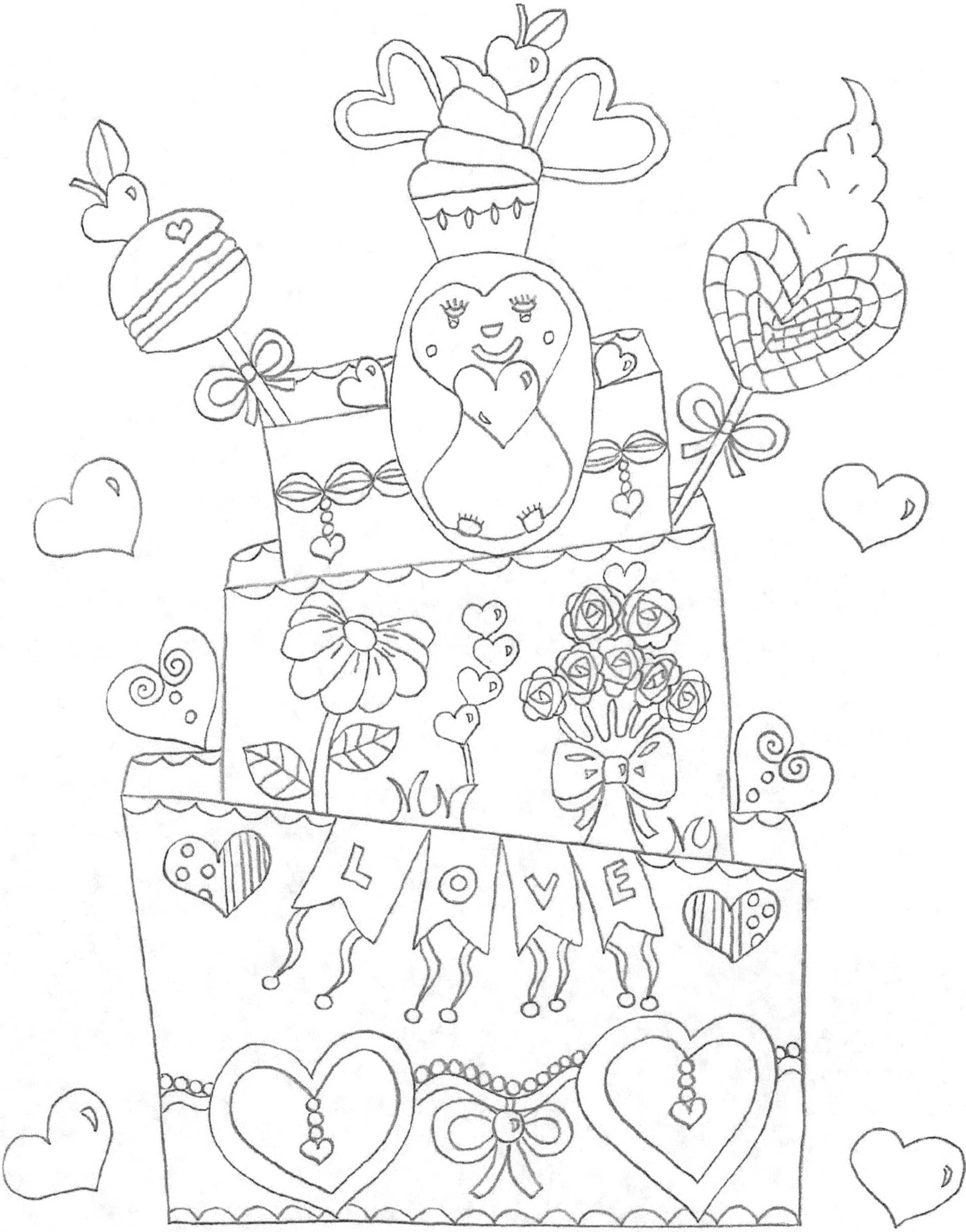
LOVE

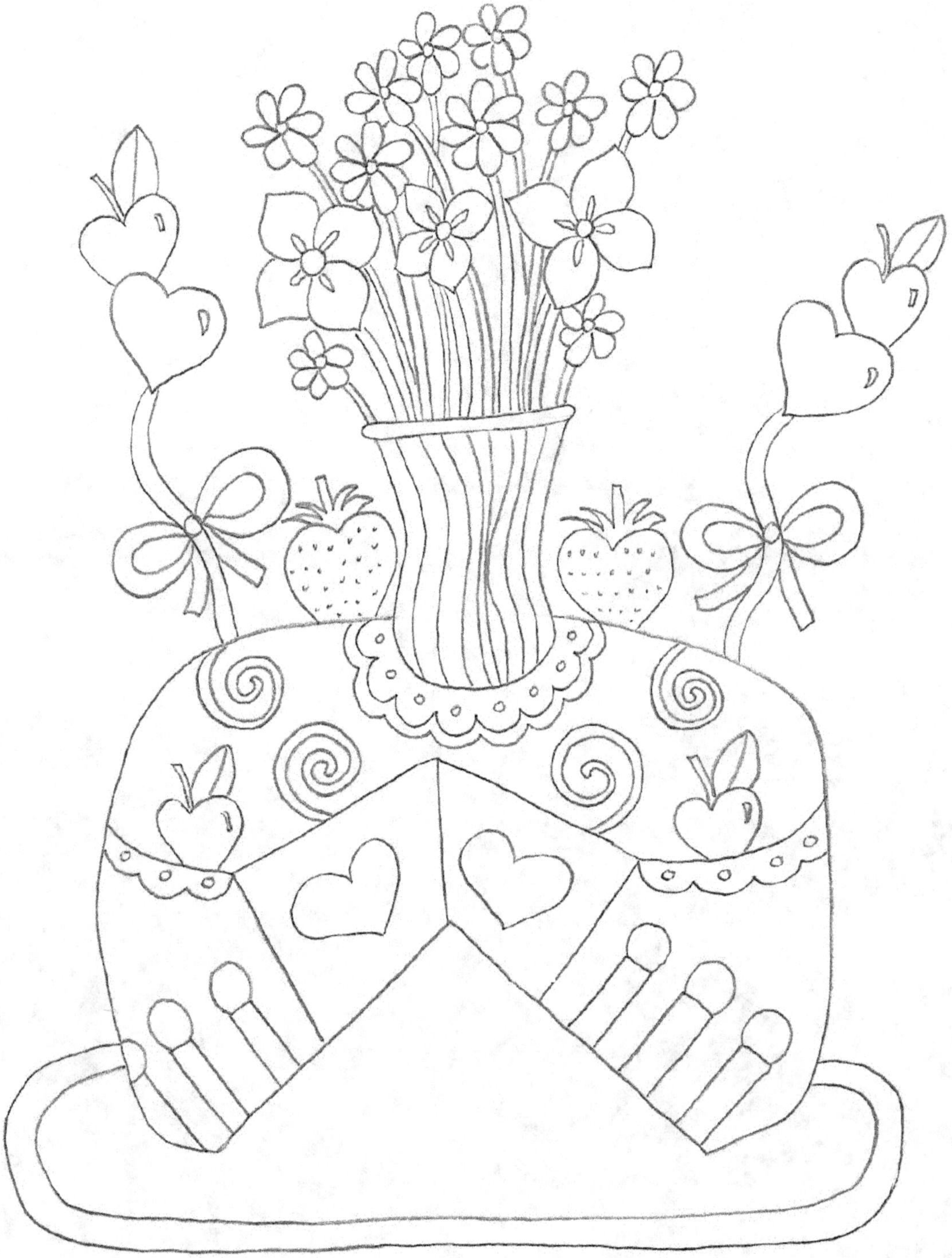

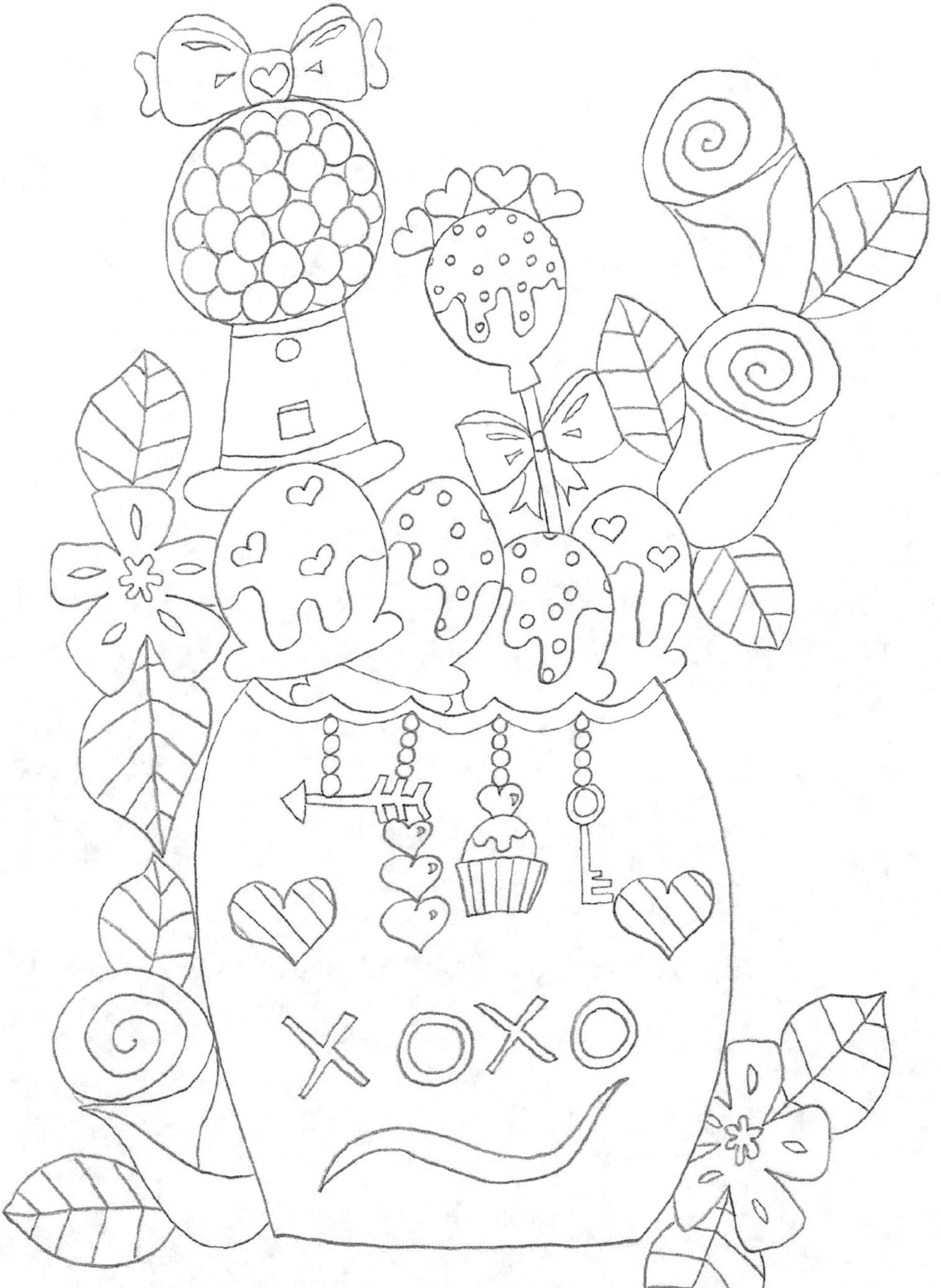
XOXO

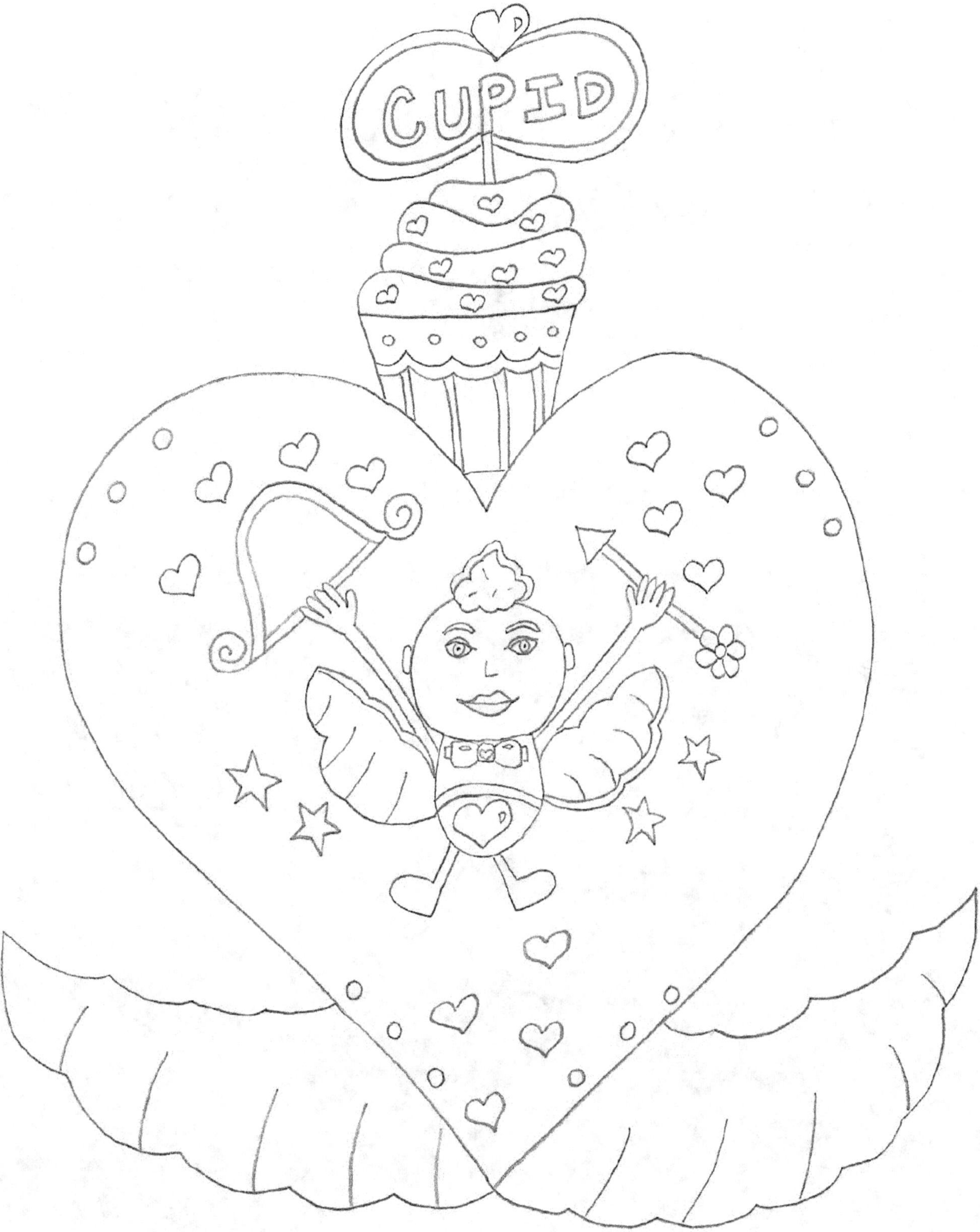
CUPID

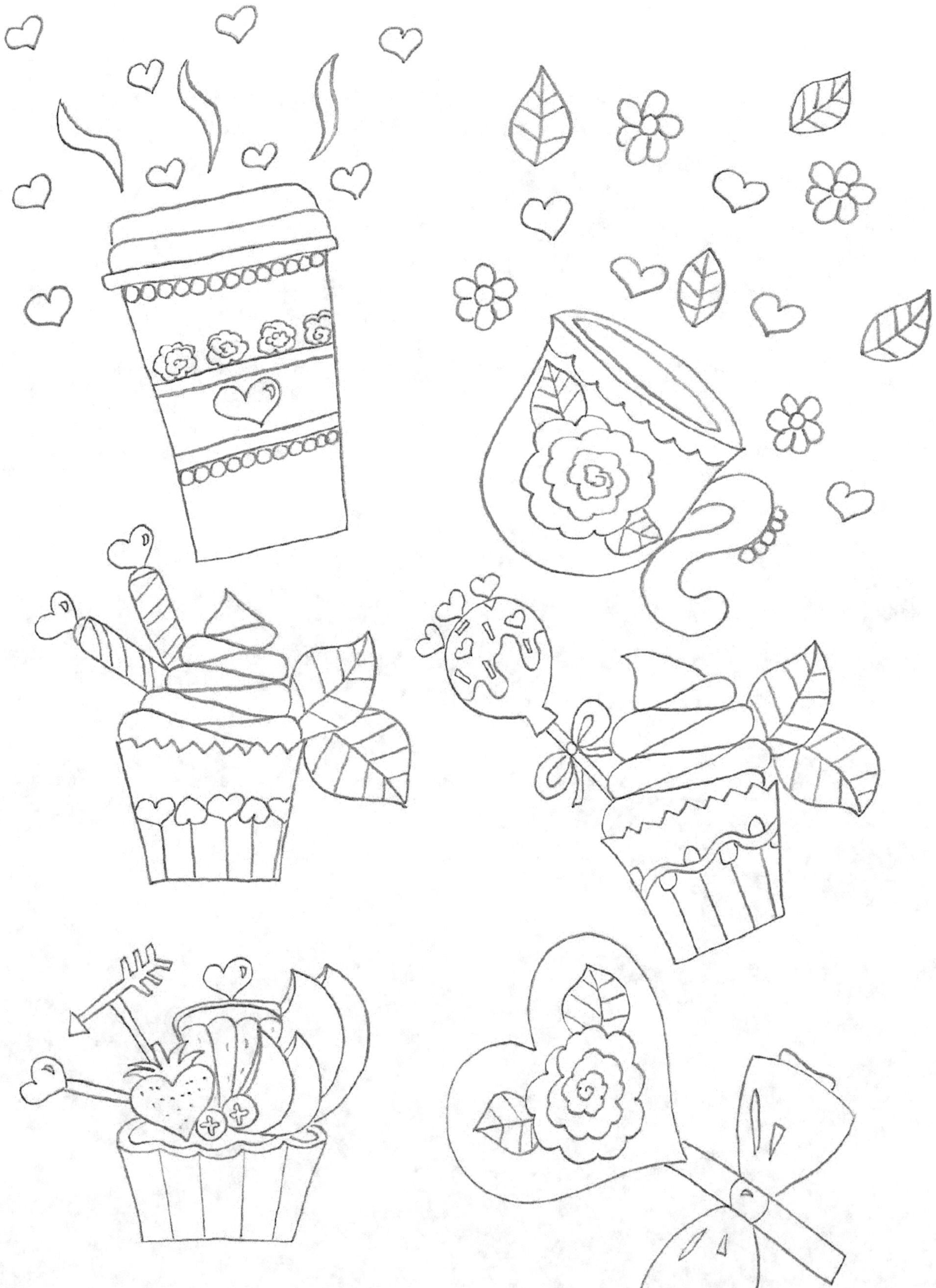

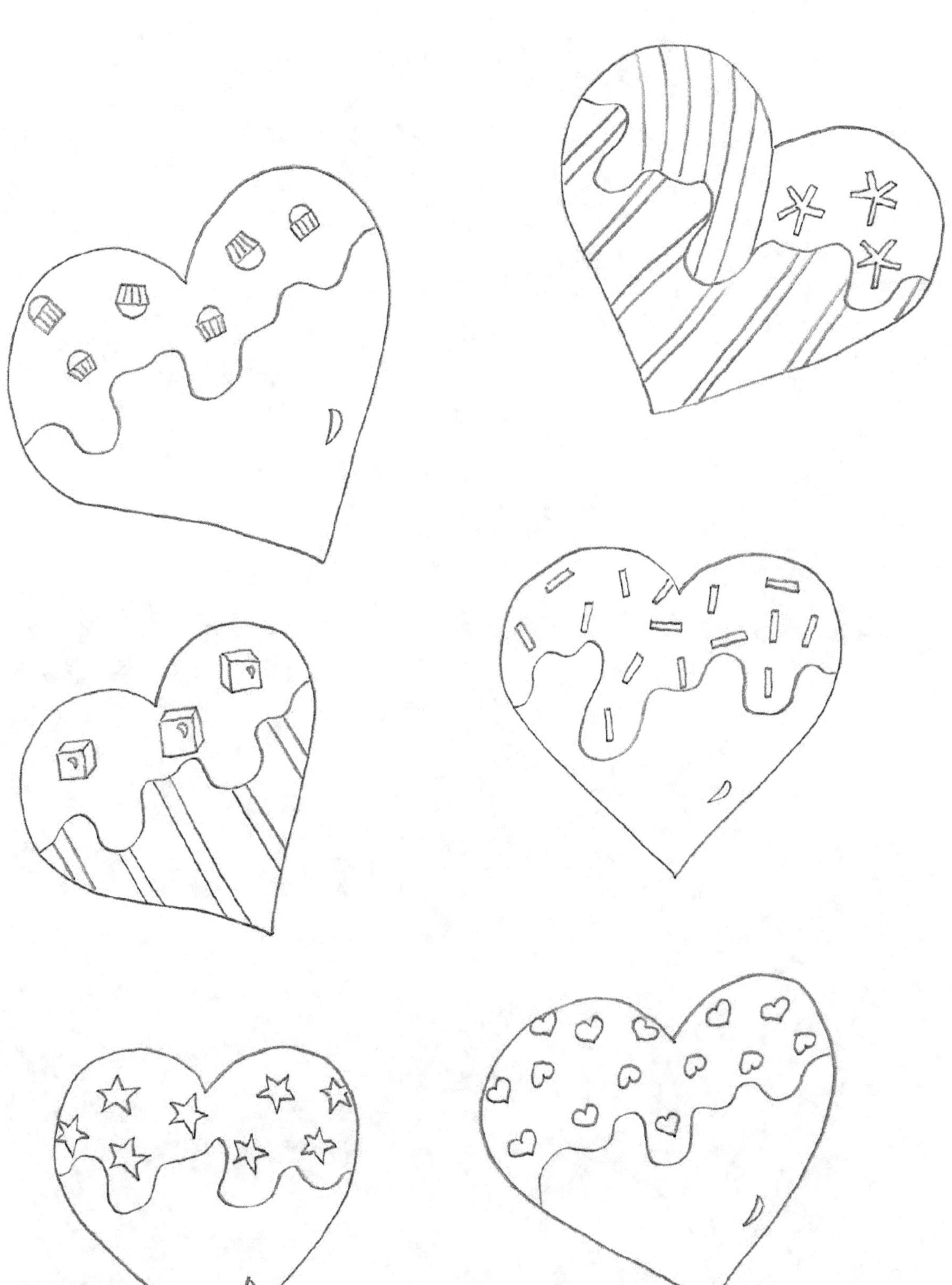

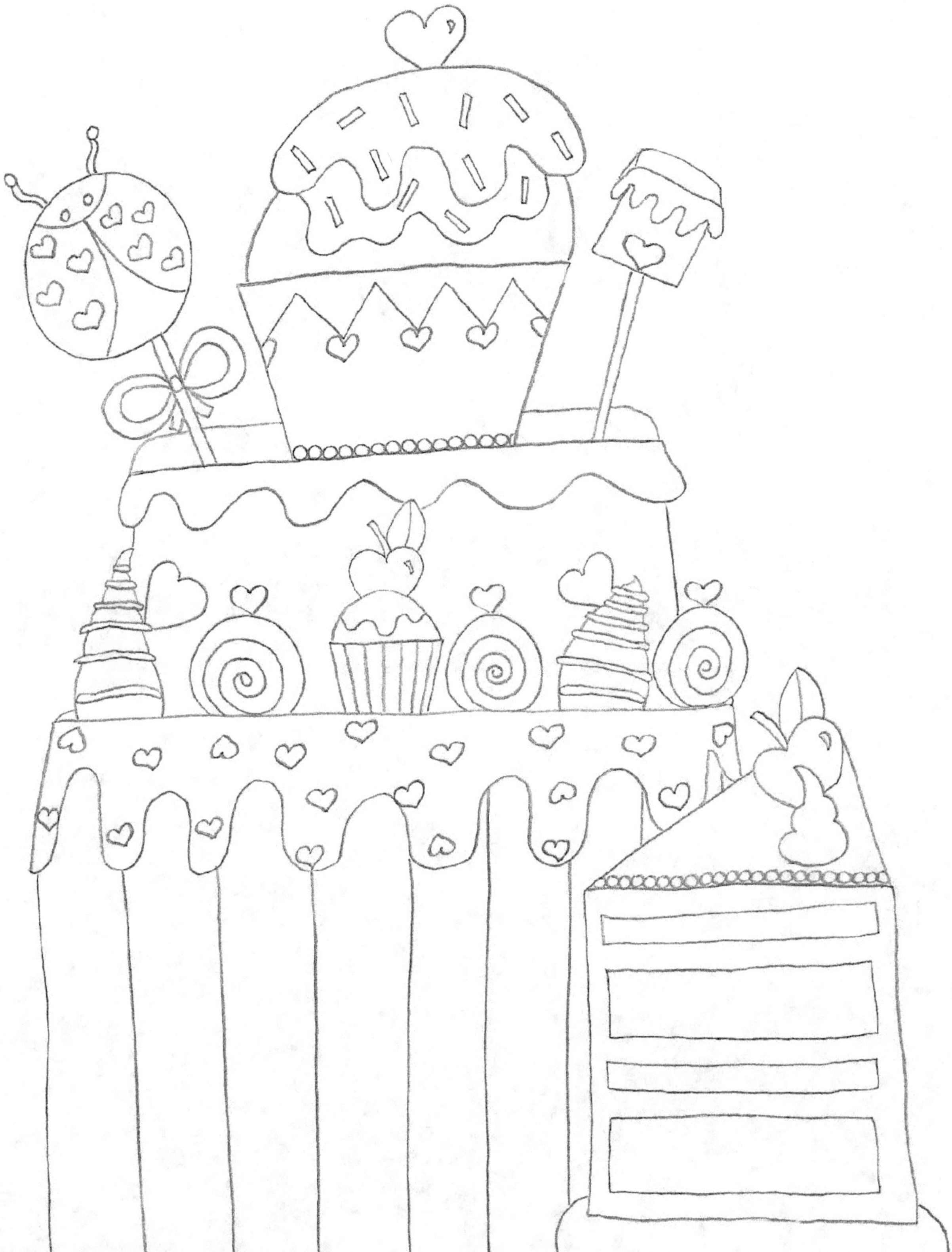

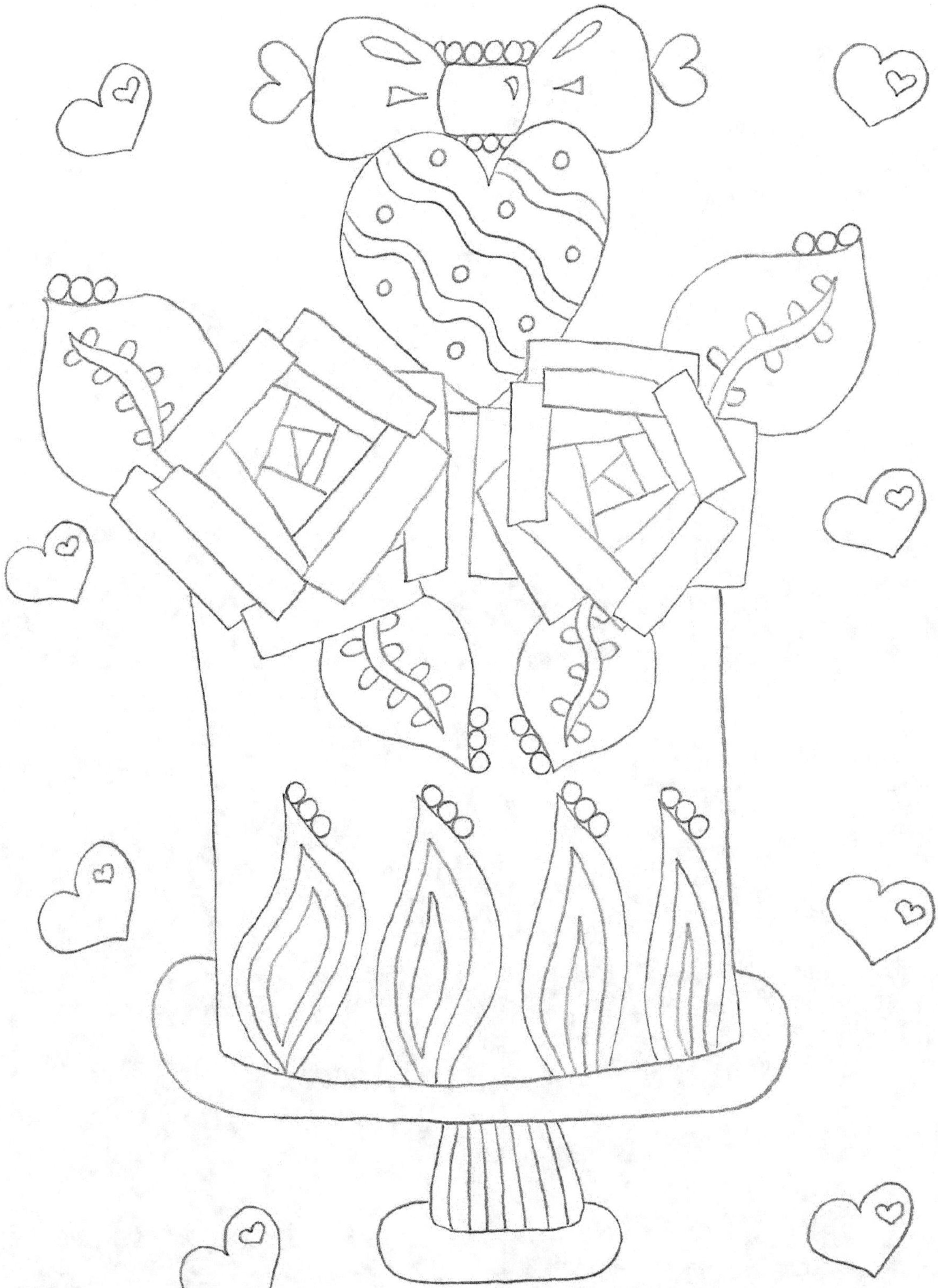

Be mine
Sweet
LOVE
Cute
XOXO
Hello

HAPPY VALENTINES
DAY

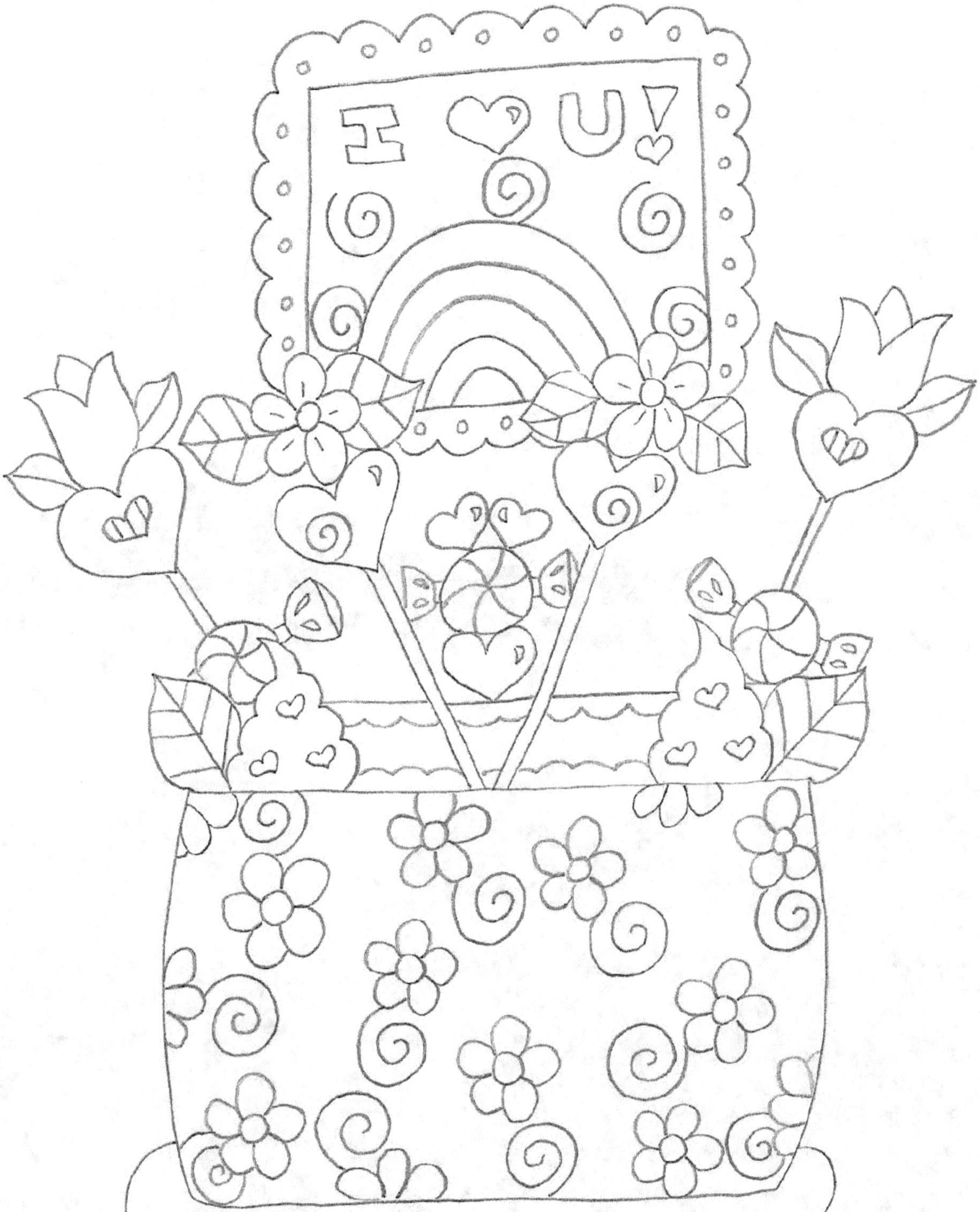
I ♥ U!

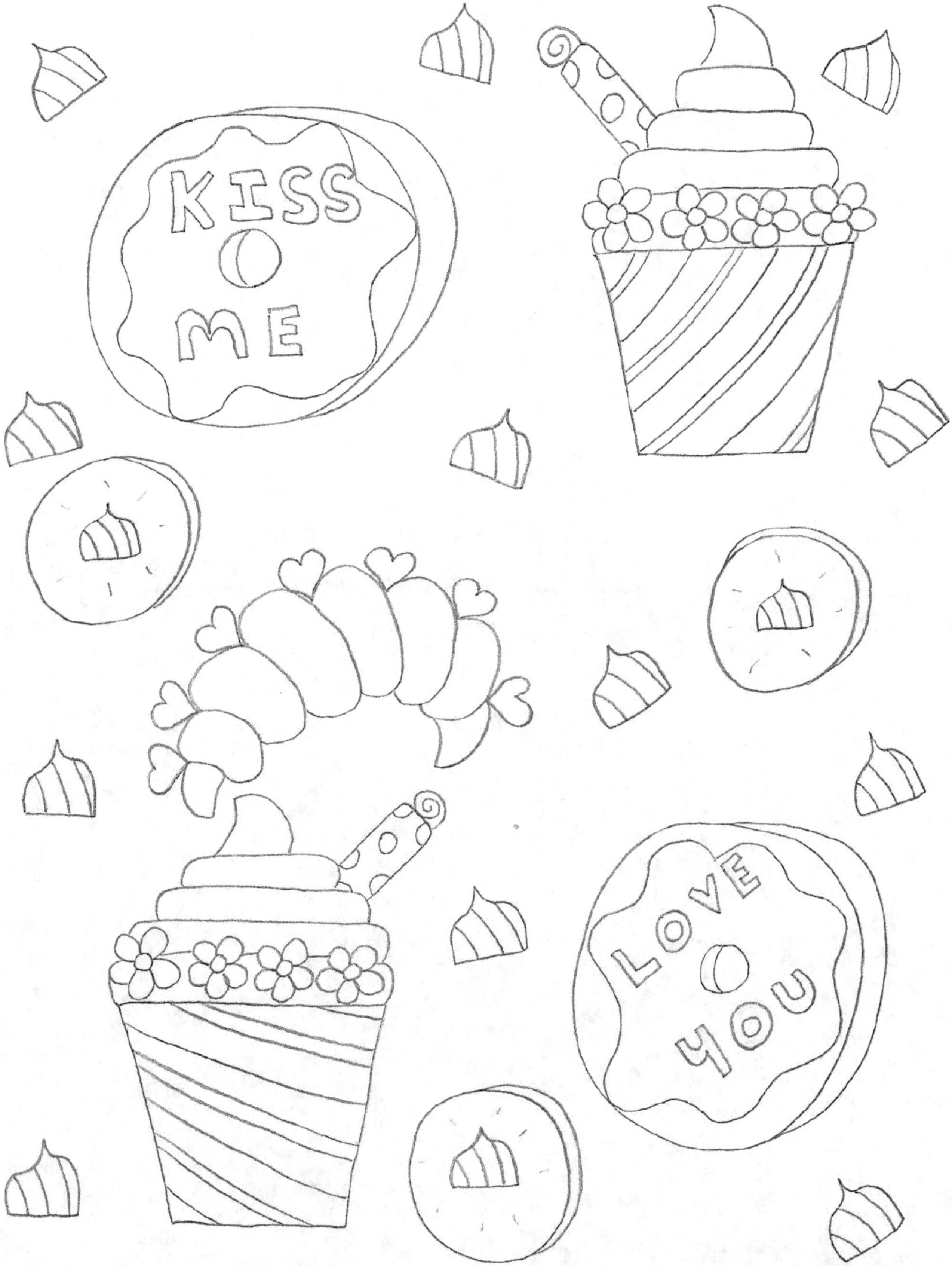
KISS
ME
LOVE
YOU

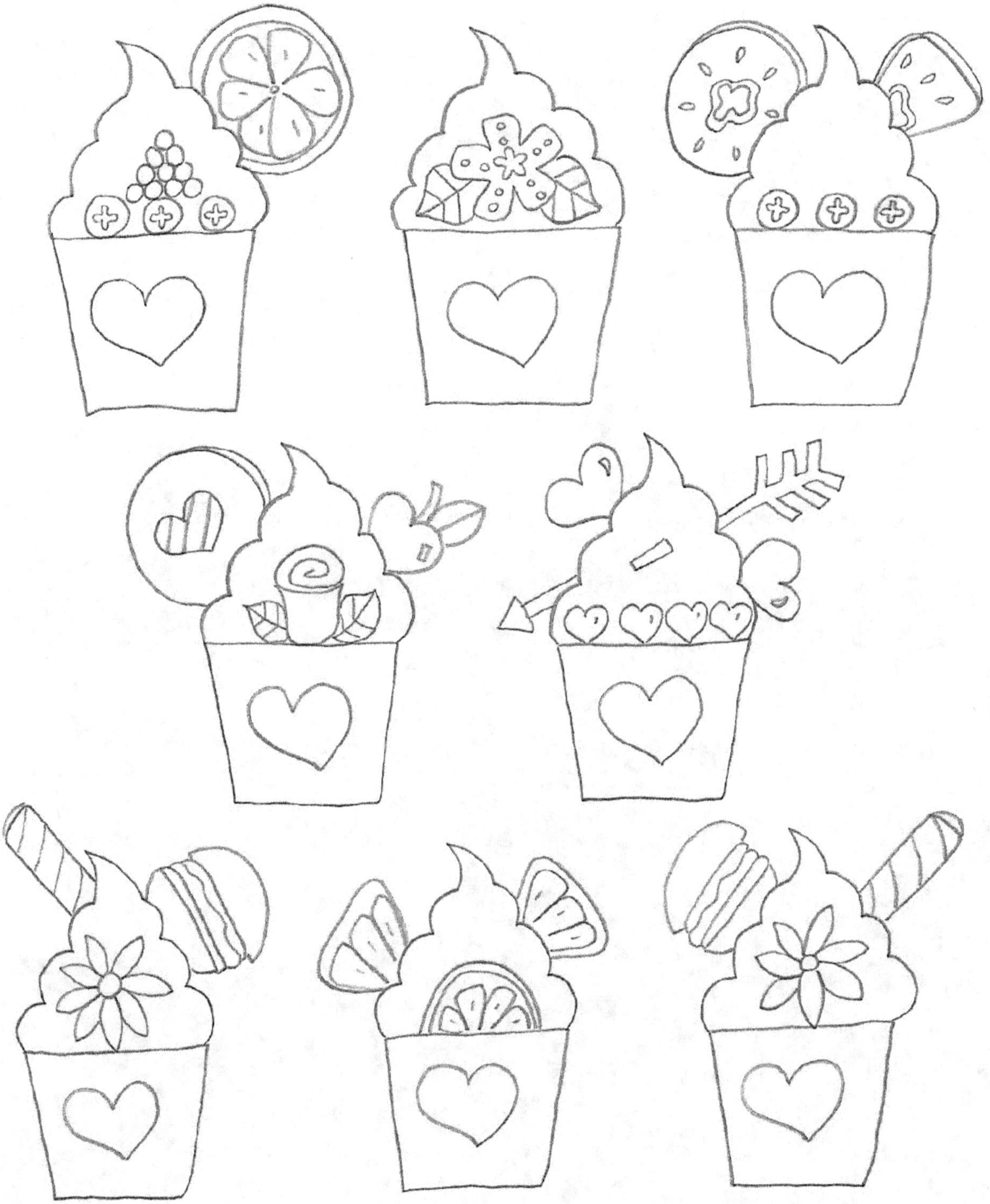

HUG
CALL ME
LOVE
XOXO
KISS

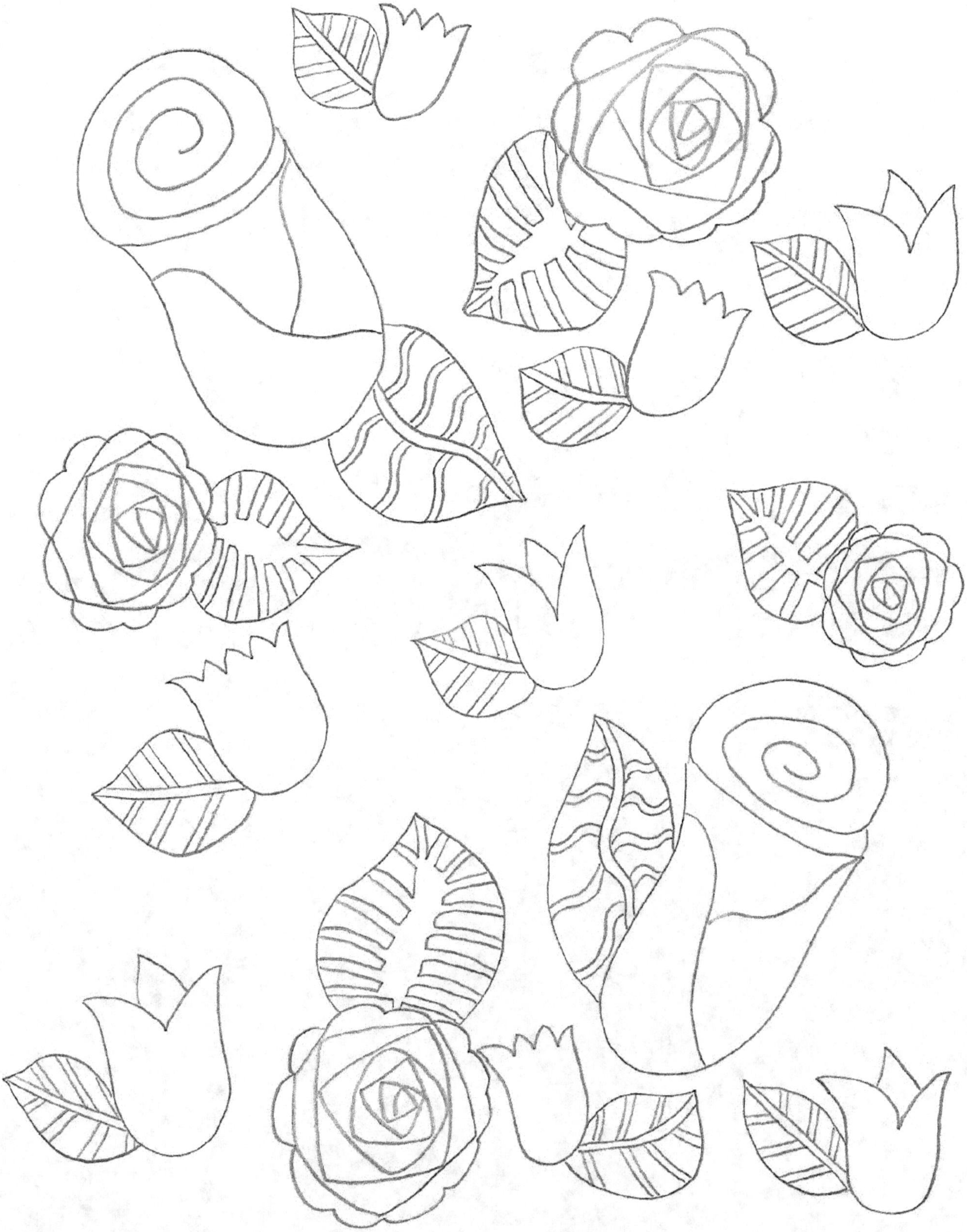

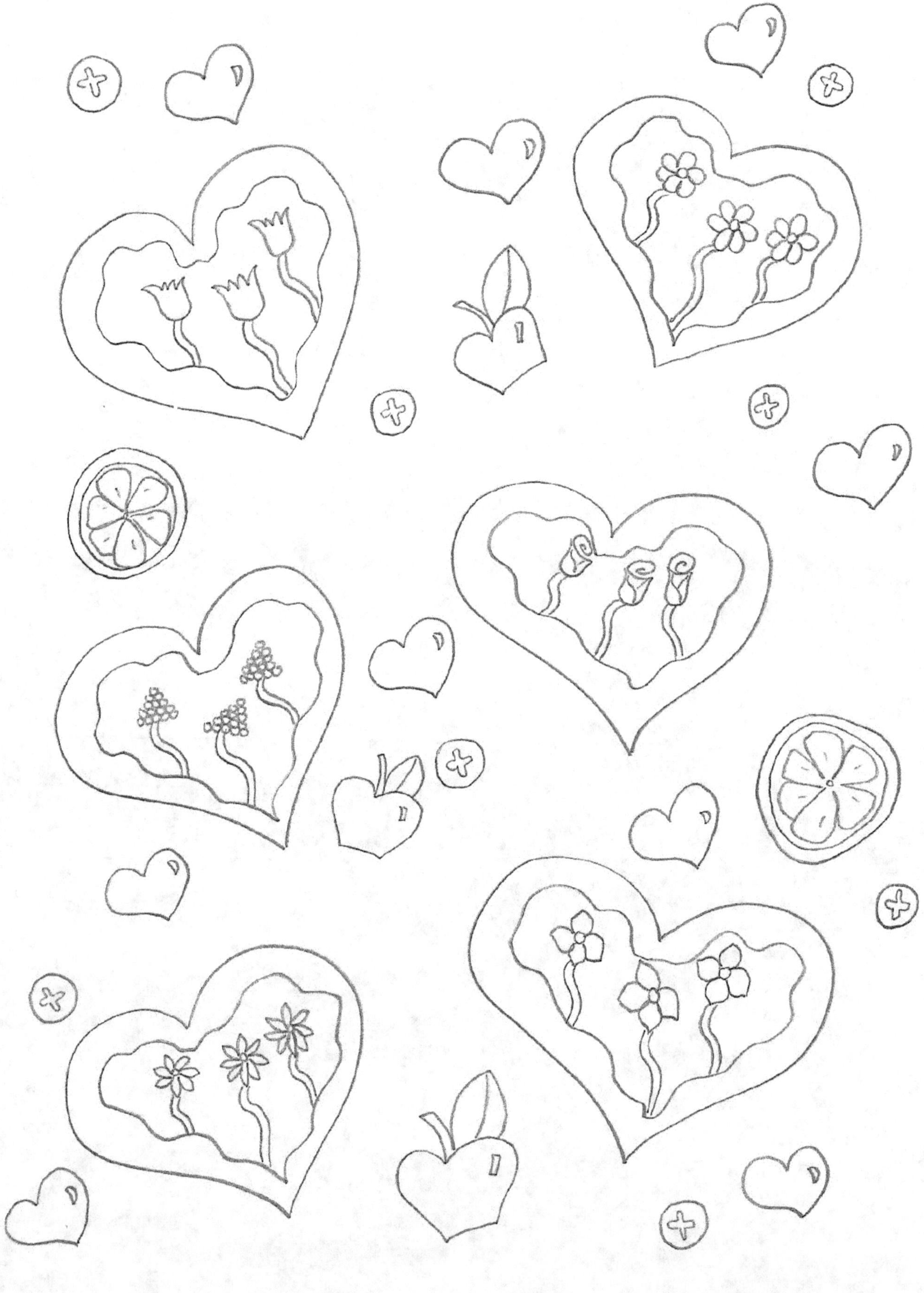

HAPPY VALENTINES DAY
Cute
XOXO
Cute
XOXO

THANK YOU FOR PURCHASING VALENTINE'S FLOWERS & DESSERTS. YOU CAN CHECK OUT MY OTHER COLORING BOOKS LISTED BELOW WHICH CAN BE PURCHASED AT AMAZON.COM:

VINTAGE PARIS BAKE SHOP (Adult)

VINTAGE WINE GARDEN (Adult)

ICE CREAM MADNESS (Adult)

ICE CREAM MADNESS VOLUME 2 (Adult)

TEA & COFFEE TROPICAL TREASURES (Adult)

TEA & COFFEE OCEAN TREASURES (Adult)

TEA & COFFEE TREASURES (Adult)

BOTANICAL FLOWERS & MANDALAS (Adult)

MAJESTIC FALL (Adult)

A VERY RETRO CHRISTMAS (Adult)

MAGICAL DESSERTS (Children)

MAGICAL DESSERTS VOLUME 2 (Children)

MAGICAL DESSERTS VOLUME 3 (Children

FASHION DOLLS (Adult)

FAIRIES IN THE FLOWER GARDEN (Adult)

MERMAID'S WONDERLAND SEA OF ENCHANTMENT (Adult)

CHRISTMAS DESSERTS

VALENTINE'S DAYDREAMS COLORING BOOK (Adult)

VALENTINE'S DAY DELIGHTS (Adult)

IF YOU ENJOYED YOUR COLORING EXPERIENCE, PLEASE TELL OTHERS ABOUT IT BY WRITING A REVIEW ON AMAZON.COM UNDER THE BOOK YOU COLORED.

www.ingramcontent.com/pod-product-compliance
Lightning Source LLC
Chambersburg PA
CBHW081629220526
45468CB00009B/2354
* 9 7 8 1 7 9 3 3 8 6 5 1 9 *